Learning Points

The idea of time is a difficult one for young children but they see how important clocks are to us and are very keen to know what they 'say'. This colourful book with detailed pictures goes through a child's day from getting up to going to bed. Each of the familiar events is related to the time on a clock face.

- Talk about the pictures together. What are the important landmarks in your child's day – and what time do they happen?

- Focus on the hours first of all, using a clock with a dial and hands.

- Before you talk about half hours, make sure your child understands what half means. Use the word when you talk together and cut apples, cakes, sandwiches into halves.

- Using this book to help you, make your own 'family time book' with a clock on each page. Encourage your child to draw appropriate pictures.

Digital faces are included as children will meet them in their daily lives.

Ladybird books are widely available, but in case of difficulty may be ordered by post or telephone from:

Ladybird Books – Cash Sales Department
Littlegate Road Paignton Devon TQ3 3BE
Telephone 0803 554761

A catalogue record for this book is available from the British Library

Published by Ladybird Books Ltd Loughborough Leicestershire UK
Ladybird Books Inc Auburn Maine 04210 USA

telling the
time

by LYNNE BRADBURY
illustrated by LYNN BREEZE

Ladybird

daytime

night-time

morning

afternoon

evening

It is 8 o'clock in the morning.

Some people are getting up.

Some people are
eating their breakfast.

At 9 o'clock
Mummy is working,
Daddy is working.

It is
10 o'clock.

Everyone is busy.

What are they doing?

It is
11 o'clock.

The children are
having a drink.

Then they go out
to play.

At 11 o'clock
grown-ups have a
drink too.

It is
12 o'clock.

12 o'clock is the
end of the morning.

12 o'clock is the middle of the day.

 At 12 o'clock
the children
are having
a meal.

Some are at home.

Some are at school.

It is 1 o'clock
in the
afternoon.

ots of people have
meal at 1 o'clock.

People eat
different things.

It is
2 o'clock.

What are these
children doing?

It is
3 o'clock.

Lots of people
like a cup of
tea at 3 o'clock.

It is
4 o'clock.

The children are
coming home
from school.

They are hungry.

At 4 o'clock the
children sometimes
watch television...

or play with their
toys.

It is
5 o'clock.

Mummy is busy.
She is cooking.

It is
6 o'clock.

These people are going home from work.

At 6 o'clock
Daddy is home.

It is
7 o'clock.

How do the children get ready for bedtime?

At 7 o'clock,
when the
children are
ready, it is
time for a story.

It is
8 o'clock.

The children are
asleep.

At 8 o'clock
Mummy is going out.
Daddy is watching
television.

8-30	9-30	10-30
half-past eight	half-past nine	half-past ten

14-30	15-30	16-30
half-past two	half-past three	half-past four